D1538551

Overcome Your Fear of Heights

How to Get Rid of Your Fear to Feel Comfortable and Have Fun

by David Bishopson

Table of Contents

Introduction

The period after a major aircraft incident such as a fatal craft or a reported hijacked plane, many of us will be cautious of travelling by air and well; perhaps, you might even feel a shiver whenever the issue of air travel comes up. This is quite normal because it is fear and fear is actually a protective human instinct. However, when it gets to a point where you would miss your best friend's wedding on the Caribbean Islands because you would have to fly there, then this is a phobia. So where do we draw the line?

A phobia is a condition where you tend to react irrationally or harbor irrational perceptions towards certain things or situations. A phobia will drive you to changing your lifestyle or certain decisions just so that you may steer clear of the perceived threat.

Many people suffer from various kinds of phobias, and though there is yet to be a solid explanation as to what causes the phobias, there is some fairly grounded speculation on the causes. One explanation states that phobias result from family background and our upbringing. How protective were your parents? Were they always telling you to stay away from the highway near your home? Was your mother fearful of dogs? Is your favorite aunt afraid of spiders?

Your experiences as a child may be what brought about your phobias but it could also be as a result of classical conditioning. This is whereby your fear of your neighbor's fierce Tibetan mastiff led to your being extremely fearful of all dogs... including leashed poodles!

This book is aimed at giving you a better understanding of your fear of heights – acrophobia; and by the time you are done reading it, there is no doubt you will be better equipped to overcome your fear.

©Copyright 2014 by LCPublifish LLC - All rights reserved.
This document is geared towards providing exact and reliable information in regards to the topic and issue covered. The publication is sold with the idea that the publisher is not required to render accounting, officially permitted, or otherwise, qualified services. If advice is necessary, legal or professional, a practiced individual in the profession should be ordered.

- From a Declaration of Principles which was accepted and approved equally by a Committee of the American Bar Association and a Committee of Publishers and Associations.

In no way is it legal to reproduce, duplicate, or transmit any part of this document in either electronic means or in printed format. Recording of this publication is strictly prohibited and any storage of this document is not allowed unless with written permission from the publisher. All rights reserved.

The information provided herein is stated to be truthful and consistent, in that any liability, in terms of inattention or otherwise, by any usage or abuse of any policies, processes, or directions contained within is the solitary and utter responsibility of the recipient reader. Under no circumstances will any legal responsibility or blame be held against the publisher for any reparation, damages, or monetary loss due to the information herein, either directly or indirectly.

Respective authors own all copyrights not held by the publisher.

The information herein is offered for informational purposes solely, and is universal as so. The presentation of the information is without contract or any type of guarantee assurance.

The trademarks that are used are without any consent, and the publication of the trademark is without permission or backing by the trademark owner. All trademarks and brands within this book are for clarifying purposes only and are the owned by the owners themselves, not affiliated with this document.

Chapter 1: What is Acrophobia?

It could be that you are afraid of heights related to certain activities, like bungee jumping, roller coaster riding, climbing mountains or even walking on footbridges that are set far above the highway. In any of these cases, you are a victim of acrophobia. Phobia comes from the Greek word *"phobos"* that means irrational fear. To be phobic is to have an unfounded fear about an object, activity or a situation.

Fear of heights is not a common occurrence for everyone. There are those who are bolder and can partake in activities that involve activities at high places. These people are said to have a head for heights because they get an adrenaline rush by doing seemingly dangerous activities. On the other hand however, we have those who deeply fear activities that are height-related and the mere thought of climbing or ascending to lofty places chills them to the bone.

Acrophobia is a term widely used to describe the fear of heights. This fear is generally exaggerated as the person may not necessarily be in a high place, of the perceived danger might be completely unfounded. While the fear of heights is intrinsic, there are people whose natural fear of heights is utterly extreme.

Only some cases of acrophobia can be explained
Sometimes, this fear has an explanation and sometimes, it just doesn't. For example, a person who has fallen off a staircase before may develop acrophobia. A person who had a loved one die or seriously injured from falling off a high place may also develop fear of heights. Whether or not you can identify why you have a fear of heights is not so important. In any case, just know this: It's manageable. It's treatable. And you can overcome it.

Some factors that can trigger the fear of heights include but are not limited to:

- Certain neurological disorders that can affect your composure and stability

- Problems maintaining your composure while standing, for example you'll see this sometimes in elderly people who have difficulty stabilizing their posture

- A temporary case of acrophobia can occur when you take some medication for which you are strictly prohibited from exposing yourself to elevated grounds

- A personal bad accident that left you wounded, scratched, or emotionally scarred, instilling a fear of heights

- Losing someone through a fatal fall thus accelerating your tragedy and fear of heights

- Fear instilled through warnings and caution from parents or guardians while growing up (i.e., your mom telling you "don't go close to the edge!" frequently)

- Tension associated with the risk of falling

- Mind triggers that initiate a false sense of falling even while you are still standing upright

- Wild imaginations brought about by hallucinations, visions and dreams

Indications that you have fear of heights

Having "a head for heights" is often applauded as being a good thing, but at times, this may not be the case. While this is considered an act of bravery or fearlessness, there are times when it can signify rebellion or bring to the surface some underlying issues such as deep-rooted insecurities or extreme cases of fighting fear. You don't need to prove anything to anyone, so overcoming your fear should solely be based on your desire to become more comfortable in fairly safe situations – not so that you can impress someone by walking a tightrope over the Grand Canyon.

Display of acrophobia on the other hand shows that your life is hindered from being what it should be since you are sentenced to live a life of fear and insecurity. People with such fears are unable to enjoy their everyday life because they tend to be mastered by the fear, are always tense, have unrealistic expectations even when they are not on high grounds, tend to be antisocial and are prone to many health risks.

Fear of heights may be a little hard to distinguish because everyone has some fear to some degree. Nonetheless, there are those that are on the extreme end of fearing heights. Such people exhibit characteristics unique to this fear like dizziness, nausea, sweating and so forth when they are ascending a footbridge or when they are in the balcony of a high house. Most likely, you already know you have an unfounded fear of heights, which is why you're reading this book. So consider yourself one step in the right direction already by recognizing that you have an issue you'd like to work on or altogether overcome. If you're still not sure, then we'll clear it up below.

Women tend to experience this fear more than men, as women tend to be more cautious. But still, anyone can be an acrophobic. Phobias are not a domain of a few specific people or one gender only, because at one time or other, events could lead to one suffering from extreme fear of some situations, activities or objects. Age is also a factor that triggers the fear of heights. While kids may be free to enjoy life and participate in height-related activities, adults may be more reserved and more skeptical.

How would you know if you fall in this category of people who have fear of heights? You may want to look out for the following signs or ask your friends to help give an accurate observation of your behavior when exposed to heights, this may be in real life situations or your reactions to pictures of tall buildings and high places.

Here is a quick checklist of indications for fear of heights:

1. A series of panic attacks when exposed to high places or even places that are not necessarily high where there is little or no protection. I remember my first panic attack was on a ski trip, about halfway down the slope of the mountain. I couldn't see the face of the mountain I was about to ski because it was beyond a little hump of snow in front of me. I completely freaked out, didn't move a muscle for about 30 minutes, and remember wanting to curl up in a ball and cry. That's a panic attack!

2. Extreme agitation, which is coupled by difficulty in descending from a high place

3. Experiencing spells of dizziness when exposed to heights – This could sometimes be accompanied by the vertigo phenomenon where you feel as if your head is spinning.

4. A serious case of anxiety that may be accompanied by shaking, crying, sweating, headaches and even fainting

5. Difficulty in breathing, wheezing sounds

6. When the mere thought of heights sends you into feverish mode

7. When you can barely look at tall buildings or edges of cliffs

8. When you cannot perform other activities that are related to steep motions for fear of falling, such as skiing

9. Prefer driving to flying

10. In extreme cases, the trigger to fear of heights may even cause you to have difficulty in waking up in the morning

Chapter 2: Five Reasons Why You Should Overcome Fear of Heights

While some people believe that fear of heights is natural and that it will go away with time, that is not the truth. If it is not treated, acrophobia will persist to old age, and if anything, it will only get worse. A new school of thought however believes that the fear of heights is as a result of many other phobias that merely manifest themselves as fear of heights.

Here are five reasons why you should overcome your fear of heights

1.   You'll be able to fulfill your life's wish list

Fear of heights will hinder you from enjoying life's simple pleasures such as boarding the plane to visit any one of the Seven Wonders of the World. To enjoy traveling experiences, climbing high structures or mountains for panoramic views may be a part of the overall full experience. Not having being able to enjoy these small pleasures in life would make you very miserable, and you'd miss out!

2.   You may also overcome other underlying problems

Everyone has a fear of heights to some extent in their life. Even infants and animals have a perception of depth and they have an innate ability to decline what they perceive not to be safe. Illogical fear of heights on the other hand is said to often be merely a manifestation of other underlying or deep-rooted problems. This may include a host of other phobias, vivid and weird imaginations or psychological issues. Overcoming your fear of heights will mean that you will be set free from such problems.

3.   There are Health Benefits to consider

Panic attacks caused by fear of heights such as agitation, swooning, and anxiety attacks could trigger serious health complications such as stroke, temporary paralysis, migraines, epileptic fit, psychological disorders and depression. You need to avert these by overcoming your fear.

4.   Avoid being exposed to other serious dangers

Although phobia for heights is not always a pleasant experience, an even bigger danger may occur when you are faced with a riskier situation and you cannot even run to safety due to your fear of heights. For example if a fire broke out in a building and the only escape was through a fire escape, your acrophobia could prevent you from going on to the fire escape, costing you your life in the process.

5. When what you fear befalls you

In Africa, they say if you fear a snake, you will always see one. If you fear heights, your chances of falling off a high place are higher than a person who doesn't fear heights. If every time you get a few feet close to the edge you shiver, you need to seek treatment.

Chapter 3: Five Important Tips to Overcome Your Fear of Heights

Is there hope for the hopelessly fearful people who fret every time they are elevated to a few feet off the ground? Of course!

1.   Perception

If you see it, you can achieve it. The first step to achieving any goal in your life is to start visualizing it in your mind. This will include having pictures of tall buildings on your vision board and imagining yourself doing things that you could not do before. The thought of you climbing tall buildings and not falling can actually become a reality in the end. Try to actually visualize yourself somewhere – for me, I use the image of picturing myself standing on top of one of the ruins in Machu Picchu, with my arms out and chest up to the sky. It's a glorious beautiful day, and I have a huge grin on my face because I'm having so much fun! (That's my visualization cue).

Scientists have proven that the part of your brain that sends out messages of fear is the same one that sends messages of safety. The thalamus is the part of the brain where all signals are relayed and sorted. The signal of fear will be sent to the amygdala where pure fear is registered.

You need to train your brain to think differently about the situation that triggers the negative response. This can be done by visualizing it until it becomes reality.

2.   See a Shrink

It is estimated that about 80% of the fear of heights experience is psychological and may be accompanied by other issues. Acrophobia may only be a symptom, but not the root cause. Experts advise that people who have such fears should not shove the problem aside but rather make efforts to see a psychologist or a therapist. You may need some form of holistic therapy so that you do not treat the symptoms only, but rather treat the root cause of the fear for heights as well.

3.   Take the edge off

Some tense emotions will occur when you are in high buildings. The last thing that you want to do is relax and take a deep breath. But do just that anyway! Go ahead, take a deep breath, and relax. There ... takes some will power, no? It is the right thing for you to do.

If you really want to overcome acrophobia, you've got to learn to just relax. Use positive affirmations regularly, telling yourself "everything's fine" and "I'm going to be ok" and "this is actually fun". Fake it until you make it (or actually believe it). Intentionally relax your muscles and body posture before you get into the plane, or before you enter the elevator. Let the tension out, all of it.

4.   Identify the triggers and avoid them

Fear of heights is sometimes triggered by a certain thing; for example, the memory of a tragedy that you cannot get out of your mind. Some people say that the feeling of the wind rushing against their face brings memories of heights. Whatever the trigger is, avoiding it will give you peace of mind. And if you can't avoid it, then at least knowing what it is can help you find another way to use the trigger. For example, instead of feeling the wind and automatically becoming scared, try really focusing your mind on how the wind feels on your face, how it's blowing through your hair and your hairs are tickling your face, and how the wind is making you feel a little cooler or cold even. Since you know the wind is your trigger, then by re-directing your thoughts about the wind – you have avoided your typical reaction. And soon enough, if you keep doing this each time you feel the wind, it will become habit or second nature to think of the positive associations of wind! As silly as this may sound, trust me: It works!

5.   Medication

In some extreme cases, medication can be recommended by your Doctor. This, in my opinion, should not be the ultimate solution or treatment. Try to work with your therapist until you overcome your fear of heights completely.

Chapter 4: The Exact Steps I Took to Overcome My Fear of Heights

While the fear of heights is not always irrational, it is not pleasant at all. That issue of being a spoilsport who opts out of the fun when you are with friends will eventually start wearing you down and it may lead to stress and depression. Many times my friends were excited to play another ski trip, and I would look for excuses not to join them, but deep down this made me very unhappy and gave me the feeling of missing out.

So what did I do about it? Simple: I decided enough is enough, and I didn't want to live within the confines of acrophobia ever again. I wanted to overcome my fear of heights, so I set out to do exactly that. And guess what: I DID. It wasn't all that hard either.

So, if you decide you want to join me here on this side (the "I'm Not Afraid of Heights Anymore" side), these are the exact things I did, and therefore I think this is exactly what you should try too:

1.   Admit you have a fear of heights

Once you admit that your fear of heights is not entirely normal, then you have made you first big step of healing. The other thing you may to try to figure out, is whether your fear of heights is triggered, innate, or justified by a specific event, experience or trauma. It is recommended that you document all the causes, the feelings and or emotions that you experience when in certain situations. Let's call this the "research" phase. And you don't have to wait until you experience things... just visualize yourself in certain situations (on an airplane, on the 75th floor of a high-rise building, in an elevator, on a ski lift, skiing down the mountain, driving along the windy cliffs on the PCH at Big Sur, etc.). Which specific scenarios make you anxious or uncomfortable?

2.   Confront the triggers of your fear + "Exposure Therapy"

After writing the causes of your fear of heights, you're going to tackle them one by one. This is called Exposure Therapy. Start small, and work your way up. Try ranking all of your triggers on a 1-10 scale (1 = slightly uncomfortable, 10 = I wouldn't do that if you paid me a million dollars). Now try to work through each of these triggers, either by actually doing the activity (with a trusted friend), or by sitting in a quiet room with your eyes closed, visualizing yourself doing them. For example, let's say your level 1 trigger is standing on a step-stool or little ladder in your kitchen to reach something out of a high cabinet. Then start there – go get your stepstool, stand on it, and remind yourself that you're perfectly fine. Do it a few times a day, for a week or two, until the activity doesn't bother you at all. You're now totally used to it, and you feel fine. Next, move to a level 2 trigger. Maybe that's the activity of going all the way out onto your balcony to the edge, and touching the guard rail with your hip. So then, do this a few times a day for a week or so. Obviously, this is easy when you can do these activities in your own home as described, but if your list has things on it like "riding on a ski lift", then you'll either need to find a local equivalent, or you can do the activities through visualizations. This is where you sit quietly in your own private space with your eyes closed, and spend time visualizing yourself on that ski lift. Do this several times a day, until you're ready to move up a level. And so on, and so on.

Also something that helps, is developing a "vision board" where you pin pictures of these scary places or activities on the vision board in your bedroom, for example, where you see them daily. Maybe you have a photo of a guy bungee jumping, or a photo of a woman skiing on a steep slope with a huge smile on her face. Make a point to look at these images regularly until your fear lessens or subsides.

3.   Use logical arguments with yourself

You may want to play down your fear of heights with logic since the fear you are experiencing is illogical. Talking yourself out of it or reviewing the facts can go a long way in helping you overcome this fear.

Also, if you have a friend or family member that is not scared of heights, who you consider to be completely rational, logical, and intelligent, then you can play the "I trust this person, they are logical, and they are not scared of this situation" game with yourself. Take that person with you out on the balcony, and when you start to get nervous, ask your logical friend: "Stacy, I'm terrified right now. Are you scared too?" When Stacy replies "no, not at all, I feel perfectly safe," then the rule of the game is: you MUST adopt her belief about the situation, and abandon your own. Tell yourself "I trust Stacy. She is smart and rational. She is my friend and would tell me if she thought this was unsafe. Because I trust her and she thinks it's safe, then so will I. This situation is safe. I am safe." Next time, you can even go out on the balcony without Stacy, again reminding yourself "Stacy doesn't think this is scary. Stacy believes this is safe. I am safe."

4.   Ease the tension

Another thing you may want to do is exercise. Working out helps your body relax. When you relax, the body will release the feel good hormones and there will not be much room for fear of anything. After working out, people feel more confident than before working out. That's a fact, so hit the gym or go for a run before you do something you know might scare you.

For some good measure, you can combine exercise with yoga and other meditation techniques will help you get some extra mental mastery of your fear and you will no longer be controlled by your fear but you will be in a position to control it.

5. Work with others

Working by yourself seems easy but it is not realistic. You will also need the help of others to win this battle. This may include visiting a therapist for starters to talk about why you have such fears and how best you can overcome them. Some may recommend medication but this is not always a solution to the problem as it only cures the immediate symptoms. You need holistic treatment to treat the root causes of the fear.

Like the AA (alcoholic anonymous) program, there are other people who have a fear of heights as you do. You are not alone, and joining such groups will help you grow out of your fear of heights and being led by a professional therapist will go a long way to ensure that you are able to dispel the dangers of heights that are conjured by your brain.

6. Know that it's a gradual process

No miracle therapy will help you overcome your acrophobia overnight, or even in a week. It will take time. But what is a few weeks or months compared to the many years of your life that you have been living in imaginary fear conjured by your brain?

Be prepared to invest time mostly, and if you want, maybe some resources too to buy books, DVDs and other affirmation material. The most important thing is small step by step progress, ensuring that each day is better than the day before and before you know it, you will be free as a bird!

Chapter 5: Positive Affirmations to Beat Fear of Heights

All human thoughts and perceptions are born in the mind and therefore it is only fair that the treatment starts there for overcoming your fear of heights.

The mind is a powerhouse. It can conjure imaginary things that can really wreck your life. Fear is one of the most detrimental effects. Start by learning how to steer your mind in the direction that you choose. In the end, you will accomplish much more than just overcoming your acrophobia.

How does making positive affirmations work?

You might already be thinking that talking to yourself and dosing your mind with positive self-statements will turn you into a loony bin case of sorts. You are wrong. Many people use self affirmations as a way to deal with fear and anxiety. Prior to giving speeches, presidents and leaders use this little trick, or musicians just before they jump onto the stage to perform, preachers do the same too.

Speaking positive thoughts into your mind is indeed calming and relaxing. Think of it this way, don't you like it when your receive compliments after a job or just someone telling you how beautiful you look? You feel good when receiving compliments because they relax the mind and release chemicals that boost your self-esteem. Many of us are belittled by our fears.

When you encounter height, irrespective of the size, you will feel overwhelmed and nervous. The thoughts running through your mind will be a resounding wave of negativity:

- "What if I fall and die?"

- "What if this building goes tumbling down?"

- "What if this banister comes lose and I fall with it?"

- "What if I lose my balance and fall over the balcony?"

- "What if.... "

Come to think of it... how many incidents have you ever come across where the balcony or balustrade comes undone and all the people leaning against it tumble down the 34 floors?

Take control of your thoughts. Instead of letting the height intimidate you by instilling irrational thoughts in you, challenge the negative energy. Tell yourself: "I have never heard of anyone who fell off this building. Why should I be the first?" "I am going to be okay, this rail is firm and strong enough to keep me from falling. I am safe." Go a step further even, and start ENJOYING the moment. Tell yourself, "Wow – look at this view – it's amazing!" Yes, the view: that's what you've been missing out on all this time focusing on the possibility of the balcony falling!

Telling yourself this will shift your focus from the negative to the positive and with your thoughts grounded, you might end up realizing your fears were baseless. Relax your mind and allow yourself gauge the situation rationally without your acrophobia coming into play.

Positive Affirmations to Fight Acrophobia

A couple of acclamations you could try include:

a) "I am okay"

b) "This is a very safe building"

c) "Nothing is going to happen to me. I am in control of the situation"

d) "I have been here before and nothing bad happened to me. I am not going to fall"

e) "The view from up here is spectacular. I am enjoying this"

f) "Rock climbing is great! I am having fun"

You may come up with your own acclamations fighting your greatest fear concerning heights. Say it out loud or just repeat it in your thoughts like a mantra. Do this every time you come across a height challenge and you will realize the fear will slowly diminish.

Chapter 6: Therapy to Overcome Acrophobia

In severe acrophobia cases, there may be the need to employ the services of a therapist who will help see you through your condition. Such severe cases may possess some extreme phobia symptoms such as:

- Excessive irrational fear to the extent you may find yourself avoiding certain situations and places.

- Your phobia interferes with your lifestyle and gets in the way of how you relate with friends and family around you.

- You begin experiencing excessive panic and anxiety even at the mere thought of very tall heights.

- Your phobia has lasted for at least 6 months.

Therapy has proven to be a very effective approach to dealing with fears and the success can be seen even after as few as 3 sessions. The key though, lies in finding a therapist that is qualified and competent enough in that particular field. It would even be a great idea to approach some of that particular therapist's previous patients and ask how efficient his/her therapy methods are.

Commonly Used Psychotherapy Approaches

1.   Desensitization

This is whereby the patient is gradually exposed to the stimuli that trigger their phobia, in this case the fear of heights. Advancements in technology have made virtual reality a particularly helpful tool in presenting the patient with a challenge in which they are several feet above ground; without being at the physical location indicated.

The therapist will start with small heights gradually increasing the heights as the patient slowly gets accustomed to various heights. This is done until eventually the acrophobe can face tall heights without panic and anxiety kicking in.

2.   Cognitive Behavioral Therapy (CBT)

This therapy method aims at changing the patient's way of thinking; as a way of dealing with their phobia. This is achieved by a series of steps:

a) Didactic component

Here, the therapist educates the patient on their acrophobia and informs them of the therapy methods used and their success rates. The aim is to make the patient enthusiastic about the treatment and instill in them positivity concerning the outcome of the therapy.

b) Cognitive component

This section of the CBT therapy aims at investigating the patient's thoughts and perceptions so as to better understand what triggers their phobia. The feelings that predispose the patient to this particular phobia are hereby established.

c) Behavioral component

The therapist then endeavors to teach the patient behavioral changes that will reverse the way they react to situations that trigger their acrophobia. This change of reaction will then see them reacting differently in the face of their fears and this is what will end their phobia.

Getting Successful Psychotherapy

One major mistake that most acrophobics make is assuming that the therapist should automatically know how to treat your condition even without your contribution. This is not the case. Your input is required just as much, so you have to be completely frank with the therapist concerning your phobia, and you have to put in some effort too. It's very different from going to a dentist where you can snooze in the chair while he does all the work.

Make sure you tell them the triggers, your reactions and your true perceptions of and feelings towards the phobia. Only then can you guarantee successful therapy that will rid you of your phobia.

Is There Drug Therapy to Diminish the Fear of Heights?

It is possible that therapy alone will prove to be ineffective for you treatment, thus potentially resulting in your doctor's recommendation of medication. The medication could be taken along side therapy or it could be used completely on its own. Normally, the former scenario applies where drugs are administered to backup the therapy. Mostly so that the drug can help you deal with therapy such as virtual reality.

The most commonly used drug classes are:

- Antidepressants
- Benzodiazepines
- Beta blockers

1.   Antidepressants

Serotonin-Specific Reuptake Inhibitors (SSRIs) and Serotonin and Norepinephrine Reuptake Inhibitors (SNRIs) are the commonly used antidepressants in treatment of phobias. They affect the levels of serotonin which essentially is a neurotransmitter responsible for one's mood and they are most often prescribed when the desensitization and CBT therapy methods fail.

These drugs do have several side effects. Of course, the kind of side effect experienced as well as its severity will largely vary from on person to the next. The most commonly expected side effects are:

- Sexual dysfunction
- Shudders

- Dry mouth
- Nausea
- Sleep disorders
- Dizziness
- Blurred vision
- Soft stool or constipation
- Acute depression or anxiety (very rarely happens but more prone to teens and children)

The drugs under this classification include: Prozac (fluoxetine), Zoloft (sertraline), Paxil (paroxetine), Luvox (fluvoxamine), Lexapro (escitalopram) and Celexa (citalopram).

2.   Benzodiazepines

These psychoactive drugs work very fast and are great for offering short-term relief of nervousness and anxiety. They should however be used with utmost care due to the risk of addiction as well as the high chances of overdosing particularly when taking the drug while drinking alcohol.

Some of the common drugs under this category are: Valium (diazepam), Ativan (lorazepam), Xanax (alprazolam) and Klonopin (clonazepam).

3. Beta blockers

By blocking adrenalin release in the body of the patient, this drug classification offers relief from the physical acrophobia symptoms. Such include increased heartbeat and trembling.

One such drug commonly prescribed is propranolol.

4. Other Drugs

One commonly used drug that does not essentially fall under the above classifications is D-cycloserine (DCS) and is normally used in conjunction with behavioral therapy. The drug is ideally used in the treatment of tuberculosis but when it comes to phobias, it works on the part of the brain known as the amygdala that is responsible for fear reflexes.

Homeopathic medicines may also be used to eliminate symptoms such as panic attacks. The idea here is to sustain inner ear balance. PureCalm™ is one such medicine.

Also, research in underway on the speculation that cortisol could help reduce acrophobia. This is a stress hormone tablet which when tested in acrophobics exhibited less anxiety and this lasted even a month after ingesting the tablet. Could this be a cure? Well, it is still too early to get excited over it, but it sure is great news to all those suffering from acrophobia. One day, the condition might just be curable by ingesting a pill.

Chapter 7: The Power of Group Support When Overcoming Fear of Heights

If it takes a village to raise a child, then it also sure does take a village to break an addiction... or a phobia in this case. You would be surprised at how therapeutic it feels to just share your feelings with someone else who can relate to your problem. Such an approach has commonly been used to break addictions and as studies have shown, the same can end phobias too.

How? Let us look at some of the basics of group support.

Basics of Group Support

1.   Guidance and counseling
Any support group should essentially be headed by a counselor and this need not be a professional. Even someone who has successfully battled and overcome acrophobia can fit the shoes. The idea is so that the rest of the team could have someone to look up to and someone who will give them hope that they too can overcome their phobia. This beacon of hope is essential.

2.   Open sharing

Group support is a safe haven for many acrophobics because there, you can share your fears and perceptions openly without being judged or treated as if you are out of your mind. If you were to tell a normal person that you fear climbing even 3 feet up, they may not get what you are so fearful about. Sharing this with people who feel the same will enable you to speak your mind freely and they may even give you tips on how to overcome your fears.

3.   Accountability partners

In a support group, you could get an accountability partner with whom you will heal together and overcome your acrophobia. The duty of the accountability partner is to see to it that you approach your fears and make progressive strides towards overcoming it. If you have someone to report to at the end of every day or week, you will have the drive to make an effort to overcome your phobia.

The accountability partner will be present to hold your hand as you face various height challenges. You can both give each other the power to overcome fear. You would be surprised at how much we human beings undermine the mere power of touch. Just knowing that someone is there for you will be a great relief.

4.   Exchanging tips

In a support group, you are better positioned to receive tips on treatment from the rest of the group members, someone could share a drug that particularly helped them fight their phobia, or another could warn the group of a certain kind of treatment, say for instance, hypnotherapy. Instead of researching from the internet, you would be getting first-hand accounts from people who have previously been in your position.

For group therapies to be successful, you have to pick a group made up of people with whom you share common interests or belong to the same social class. You see, you have to feel comfortable and free with all attendants and such would not really be possible when you are in a group of people you do not like.

Chapter 8: Your Confidence is Back, Now Go and Face the Heights!

The thing about phobias is that they belittle us, making us feel helpless and they tamper with our perceptions such that even a little height feels like a couple of miles off the ground. Your lifestyle may be changed depending on the development of your phobia and it may even have gotten in the way of your relationships, your friendships and your work. Imagine having to turn down a lucrative job just because its office is on the 42nd floor!

You Can Now Challenge Heights

Now that you have read some of the tips that will help you deal with your phobia, you can emerge from your shell and start living a normal life. You can go hiking or rock climbing now and breathe in the fresh unpolluted air at high altitudes. This is not to say you might not feel some fear. Fear is a normal part of all humans, it is what keeps us alive and sane in many instances, but now your fear will be rational. You will no longer stand at the edge of a reef by the beach and start sweating and trembling. Your heart will no longer start pounding hard when you are walking or driving over a bridge.

Perhaps now you can stop postponing that long overdue visit you owe your friend and ride the elevator on up to their office on the 50th floor and give him a surprise visit. You have nothing to fear now. You have overcome your phobia and at this exact moment, you realize you are bigger than you tremors... bigger than your dizziness... bigger than your panic.

You can now go on a hot air balloon ride an it will not be scary. You can now ride the scary rollercoaster and you may even throw up at the end from motion sickness, but you will not start shaking like a frail leaf from a fear of heights. Can you feel your heartbeat now...? It will no longer fail you when you are leaning over a balcony. I bet even by now, you probably realize that you will not fall off.

Take One Step at a Time

The building will not suddenly crumble; the banister will not suddenly fail and come loose. You are fine; these are all distant fantasy memories now, like a horrible nightmare that has finally ended. You have followed all the treatment tips, you feel your condition getting better... do not worry if you still cannot at once just get up and climb Mt. Everest. It will take some time to get used to open heights but now that you can comfortably look out of the window of a tall building, that's a good start.

Conclusion

You have been holed up for so long and I bet by now you are eager to catch up on all that you have been missing out on all the time that your phobia had been engulfing you. If you still need some treatment, do not feel disheartened, your acrophobia may take some time to go away but this does not mean that it won't, eventually.

You might still have to repeat your self-acclamation mantras or visualization exercises every so often. You might still have to take some medication right before you start hiking a mountain. You might still need to talk to a therapist before you go bungee jumping, but look at the bright side: you can do all those things now. You can spread your wings and experience the beauty hidden in tall heights.

Take one day at a time... one step at a time. If you feel a panic attack coming on when the hot air balloon is at an altitude of 1800m, let the instructor know and he will reduce the height at which you are cruising. You are healed now, take that in and do not beat yourself up if some things will require more time for you to get accustomed to. At least you have started on the path of recovery and that feeling of accomplishment is beyond words.

Thank you and good luck! Oh also, if you enjoyed this book, please take time to share your thoughts and post a review on Amazon. It'd be greatly appreciated!

86039424R00035

Made in the USA
Lexington, KY
07 April 2018